FORBES' PARAKEET
Threatened: Nationally endangered
(250–1000 adults)

CHATHAM ISLAND MOLLYMAWK
At Risk: Naturally uncommon

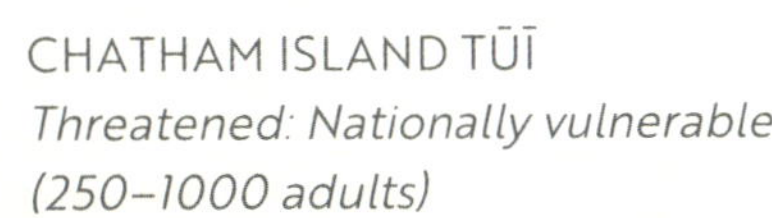

CHATHAM ISLAND TŪĪ
Threatened: Nationally vulnerable
(250–1000 adults)

BLACK ROBIN
Threatened: Nationally critical
(less than 250 adults)

TŌREA TAI/CHATHAM ISLAND OYSTERCATCHER
Threatened: Nationally critical
(less than 250 adults)

CHATHAM ISLAND SNIPE
Threatened: Nationally vulnerable
(1000–5000 adults)

One Weka Went Walking

Chatham Islands/Wharekauri/Rēkohu

One Weka Went Walking

Written by Kate Preece

Illustrated by Pippa Ensor

One weka went walking, out to explore
his Chatham Island home, from the trees to the shore.
Out of his egg, for two months at best,
he longed to know what lay beyond his cup nest.
With a twitch of his tail he set off to find friends.
Let's follow along, to see how it ends.

Fact: In 1905, 12 buff wekas were released on Chatham Island.
Today, there are tens of thousands living there.

One weka went walking and what did he see?
A rather plump pigeon, high up in a tree.
'What is your name?' Weka called from the ground.
'Parea,' said he, with a deep cooing sound.
'My cousin is Kererū, though he's a bit thinner,'
he said between mouthfuls of hoho fruit dinner.

Fact: The parea is among the world's largest pigeons. Weighing more than a loaf of bread, the Chatham Island pigeon is a packet of biscuits heavier than the New Zealand wood pigeon/kererū.

One weka went walking and what did he hear?
Two tūī talking, one far and one near.
Their words formed a song that echoed around,
telling tales of the bounty of food they had found.
While Weka watched, they sipped nectar from flowers,
as pollen and seed fell about them in showers.

Fact: The Chatham Island tūī eats nectar, fruit and insects. It has an important role pollinating and spreading the seeds of native plants.

One weka went walking and what did he eat?
The crunchy brown wētā that fell at his feet.
A tiny black robin puffed out her chest
and went looking for what had escaped her neat nest.
'That wasn't your kai, you cheeky wee bird!
I have children to raise, haven't you heard?'

Fact: In 1980, Old Blue was one of only five black robins left in the world. With some human help, she was able to raise the first of many black robin families that live there now.

One weka went walking and what did he touch?
Soft feathers of green, three in a clutch.
It was then that he noticed a pretty green face,
'Parakeets here? In this windy place?'
'We're two of a kind – and royal,' Forbes said,
'Some crowns are yellow and others are red.'

Fact: The Forbes' parakeet lives on the uninhabited Mangere/Maung' Rē and Little Mangere/Tapuaenuku islands and has a bright yellow crown, distinguishing it from the Chatham Island red-crowned parakeet.

One weka went walking and what did he spy?
A bird with fluorescent green splashed on his eye.
This super-cool bird, with a mohawk in black,
had dots that connected his neck to his back.
The Pitt Island shag enjoys life on the rocks,
eating and sleeping on jagged outcrops.

Fact: Both endangered species, the Pitt Island and Chatham Island shags look quite different from each other. The black and white Chatham Island shag has orange patches on its face.

One weka went walking and what did he view?
A one-legged bird standing out in the blue.
Tōrea tai, with gymnastic precision,
then smoothly and steadily swapped her position.
'A foot tucked away from the Antarctic chill
is easily warmer,' she said through clenched bill.

Fact: The oldest Chatham Island oystercatcher/tōrea tai was over 30 years old!

One weka went walking and what did he wish?
To join in the mollymawk's hunt for fresh fish.
With a serious look on her black-and-white face,
her wide-stretching wings skimmed the water with grace.
Slender grey feathers left lines in the sea,
as she glided along, effortlessly.

Fact: The Chatham Island mollymawk is a rare albatross, which breeds on The Pyramid/Tarakoikoia/Tcharako, but otherwise leads a life at sea.

One weka went walking and what did he spot?
A bird like a kiwi, but one that was not.
'I'm a snipe,' said the bird, long-billed and round.
'Of my kind I'm the smallest, but I make a loud sound.'
The leaf litter rustled as he probed it at pace,
seeking a beetle of exceptional taste.

Fact: As long as a pencil and lighter than a bar of soap, the Chatham Island snipe is the smallest snipe in the southern hemisphere.

One weka went walking and what did he say?
'That sounds like the warbler . . . where are you today?'
The pale-coloured songbird, caught by surprise,
looked down at the weka with little red eyes.
'I can't move, I'm afraid. A cuckoo is near.
She'll put eggs in my nest, and then disappear.'

Fact: Shining cuckoos, although rare on the Chatham Islands, are known for sneaking their eggs into Chatham Island warbler nests. Once the cuckoo hatches, it kicks the other eggs or chicks out of the nest.

One weka went walking and what did he snatch?
The start of a song he never could match.
The melodious singer, with notes on repeat
came down through the trees to land at his feet.
'That's black robin's friend!' Weka realised at last.
The tiny tomtit, gold-chested and fast.

Fact: The Chatham Island tomtit helped save the black robin from extinction by fostering Old Blue's eggs.

One weka went walking and what did he get?
The chance to see tāiko without getting wet.
From a burrow carved deeply in dark, peaty ground,
she climbed up a tree till a launchpad was found.
As she took to the air, Weka thought, 'What a treat,
to see this bird off on her winter retreat.'

Fact: The Chatham Island tāiko/magenta petrel was believed to be extinct until 1978. It is one of the world's rarest seabirds.

One weka went walking and what did he find?
A wide range of birds that are one of a kind.
'These islands are home to some species so rare,
we're lucky to see them and that they're still here.'
With a screech that was made with all of his might
Buff Weka was gone, deep into the night.

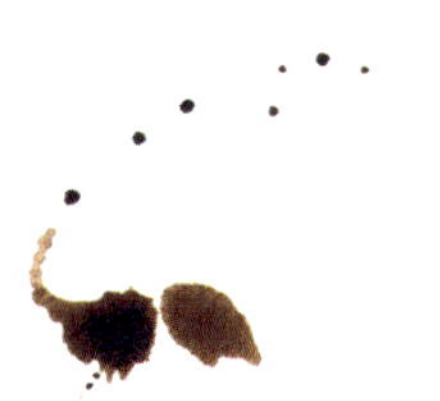

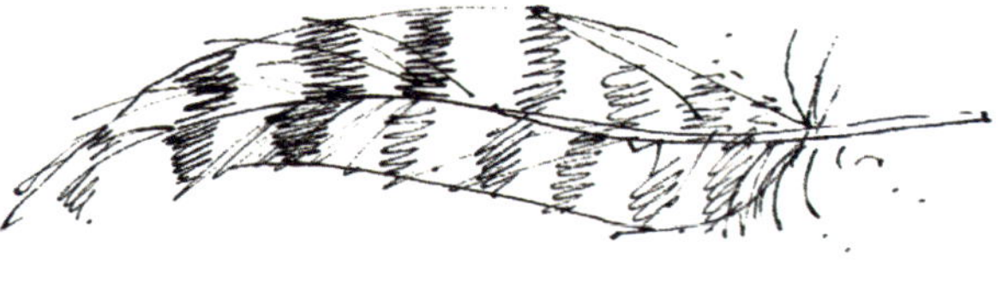

Fact: While mainland New Zealanders are known as Kiwis, Chatham Islanders call themselves Wekas.

For Ava, Henry, Edith & Patric

This book is mostly written in English. Māori translations sometimes appear after the word, and occasionally Moriori too.

Published in 2022 by David Bateman Ltd,
Unit 2/5 Workspace Drive, Hobsonville,
Auckland 0618, New Zealand
www.batemanbooks.co.nz
ISBN: 978-1-77689-012-5

A catalogue record for this book is available from the National Library of New Zealand.

Book design: Vida Kelly
Printed in China by Toppan Leefung Printing Ltd

SOURCES

Robertson, Hugh A., Baird, Karen A., Elliott, Graeme P., Hitchmough, Rodney A., McArthur, Nikki J., Makan, Troy D., Miskelly, Colin M., O'Donnell, Colin F. J., Sagar, Paul M., Scofield, R. Paul, Taylor, Graeme A., & Michel, Pascale (2021). *New Zealand Threat Classification Series 36: Conservation status of birds in Aotearoa New Zealand, 2021.* Department of Conservation Te Papa Atawhai.
Department of Conservation Te Papa Atawhai, www.doc.govt.nz
New Zealand Birds Online: The digital encyclopaedia of New Zealand birds, www.nzbirdsonline.org.nz

BUFF WEKA
At Risk: Relict
(more than 20,000 adults)

CHATHAM ISLAND WARBLER
At Risk: Naturally uncommon

CHATHAM ISLAND TOMTIT
Threatened: Nationally endangered
(250–1000 adults)

PAREA/CHATHAM ISLAND PIGEON
Threatened: Nationally vulnerable
(250–1000 adults)

CHATHAM ISLAND TĀIKO/MAGENTA PETREL
Threatened: Nationally critical
(less than 250 adults)

PITT ISLAND SHAG
Threatened: Nationally vulnerable
(1000–5000 adults)